Who Is
Bill Gates?

W0231692

Who Is
Bill Gates?

by Patricia Brennan Demuth

illustrated by Ted Hammond

Penguin Workshop

For Rite, my sister of generous heart and musical soul—PBD
For Stephanie and Jason—TH

PENGUIN WORKSHOP
An Imprint of Penguin Random House LLC, New York

Text copyright © 2013 by Patricia Brennan.
Illustrations copyright © 2013 by Ted Hammond.
Cover illustration copyright © 2013 by Penguin Random House LLC. All rights reserved.
Published by Penguin Workshop, an imprint of Penguin Random House LLC, New York.
PENGUIN and PENGUIN WORKSHOP are trademarks of Penguin Books Ltd.
WHO HQ & Design is a registered trademark of Penguin Random House LLC.
Manufactured in China.

Visit us online at www.penguinrandomhouse.com.

Library of Congress Control Number: 2012019975

ISBN 9780448463322   10 9 8 7 6 5 4 3 2

Part of the *What Is Science & Technology?* Boxed Set, ISBN 9780593090138

Contents

Who Is
Bill Gates?

In 1980, some businessmen arrived at a small company named Microsoft. They had come to meet the president, a man named Bill Gates.

Dressed in suits, white shirts, and ties, and carrying briefcases, the men looked important.

And they were. They were executives from IBM (International Business Machines). At that time IBM was the largest maker of computers in the world.

When a young guy showed up, the men asked him the way to Bill Gates's office. The guy led them there. A moment later, he took his seat behind the desk! He was Bill Gates, the head of Microsoft!

At that time, Bill Gates was just twenty-four years old. He looked even younger. His mop of hair, owl glasses, freckles, and pullover sweater

made him look like a teenager. But once Bill started talking, the IBM men were impressed. They could see that Bill knew computers—inside and out.

The computers that IBM made were huge. Some of them took up entire rooms! Big companies and government departments bought them. Very few people had personal computers. Small computers were just starting to be made. That's why IBM was visiting Microsoft. It was a young company that specialized in small computers.

Before long, IBM made a deal with Bill Gates and Microsoft. He didn't know it then, but the deal with IBM would start a whole new era in the world of computers. It would also lead to Bill becoming the richest man on earth.

Chapter 1
Young Thinker

William Henry Gates III was born on October 28, 1955, in Seattle, Washington. Because he was the third Gates male to be named William Henry, the family nicknamed him Trey. *Trey* is a cardplayer's term for *three*. Everyone else called him Bill.

Bill was a very active child. He would rock for hours on his rocking horse. Back and forth. Back and forth. Years later in business meetings, Bill was known for rocking back and forth in his chair. He said it helped him think.

Bill's parents were educated and well-to-do. William Gates Sr. was a successful lawyer. Mary Gates was a schoolteacher. After her children were born, she cared for her kids and did a lot of volunteer work. Smart and outgoing, Mary often took young Bill along with her on volunteer outings.

The Gateses were a warm and close family. Bill's sister Kristi was two years older and his sister Libby was nine years younger.

On school nights, no TV was allowed. Instead, the Gates family talked, played games, and read books.

Bill was a hungry reader. At age seven, he decided to read the entire encyclopedia! He read his way through all of *World Book*!

Anyone could see that young Bill was very smart. For Bill, thinking was an activity like drawing or reading. Once the whole family—except Bill—was in the car, ready to go on a short trip. "Where's Bill?" asked Kristi. When his mother went back inside and found him, she said, "Bill, what are you *doing*?" Bill explained, "I'm *thinking*, Mother!"

Bill always looked for ways to challenge himself. He was left-handed. If he was bored in school, he took notes with his right hand.

When he was eleven, Bill entered a contest at his church. Any kid who could memorize the Sermon on the Mount got to have dinner at a restaurant at the top of the famous Space Needle in Seattle. The Sermon on the Mount is a long Bible passage. It would fill seventeen full pages in this book. Bill learned it all by heart and amazed the minister. Bill was the only one who didn't make a mistake. "I couldn't believe that an eleven-year-old boy had that kind of mind," the minister said. Bill told the minister matter-of-factly, "I can do anything I set my mind to."

Winning mattered a lot to Bill. He hated losing—at anything. Each summer, the Gates family stayed two weeks at a cabin on Hood Canal, near Puget Sound. The place was called Cheerio. Lots of other young families went to Cheerio, too. Weeks there were filled with fun, sports, and games. Every year the kids held their own "Olympics."

All the kids wanted Bill on their team. Just
because he was smart and used big words didn't
mean he wasn't good at sports. Bill was small in
size, but he made up for it in pure grit. No matter
what he did, Bill gave his all.

SEATTLE AND THE SPACE NEEDLE

SEATTLE, IN THE STATE OF WASHINGTON, IS THE LARGEST CITY IN THE PACIFIC NORTHWEST, WITH A POPULATION OF MORE THAN SIX HUNDRED THOUSAND PEOPLE. IT IS A BEAUTIFUL CITY, SURROUNDED BY

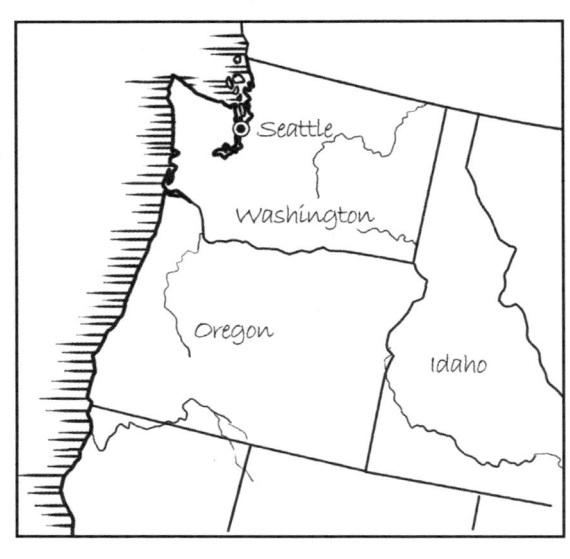

MOUNTAINS AND WATER. IT LIES ON PUGET SOUND, AN ARM OF THE PACIFIC OCEAN.

AT THE END OF THE NINETEENTH CENTURY, SEATTLE BECAME A GATEWAY NORTH TO ALASKA AFTER GOLD WAS FOUND NEAR THE KLONDIKE RIVER. THOUSANDS OF PEOPLE LEFT HOPING TO STRIKE GOLD AND GET RICH QUICK. ALMOST A CENTURY LATER, THE CITY DEVELOPED INTO A MAJOR TECHNOLOGY CENTER AFTER THE MICROSOFT CORPORATION MOVED THERE FROM ALBUQUERQUE, NEW MEXICO, IN 1979. BILL GATES IS SEATTLE'S MOST FAMOUS NATIVE CITIZEN.

IN 1962, SEATTLE HOSTED A WORLD'S FAIR CALLED CENTURY 21. IT GAVE VISITORS (INCLUDING SIX-YEAR-OLD BILL GATES) A GLIMPSE INTO THE WONDERS OF THE FUTURE. ONE OF THE FAIR'S MAIN ATTRACTIONS WAS THE SPACE NEEDLE, WHICH STILL STANDS TODAY AS SEATTLE'S MOST FAMOUS LANDMARK. IT WAS BUILT TO WITHSTAND WINDS AS HIGH AS TWO HUNDRED MILES AN HOUR AND EARTHQUAKES THAT REACH 9.1 ON THE RICHTER SCALE.

THE SPACE NEEDLE LOOKS SOMETHING LIKE A FLYING SAUCER HOVERING MORE THAN FIVE HUNDRED FEET ABOVE THE CITY. THE ELEVATOR RIDE UP TO THE OBSERVATION DECK TAKES LESS THAN A MINUTE—BUT WAITING IN LINE FOR THE ELEVATOR CAN TAKE HOURS! FROM THE OBSERVATION DECK OR INSIDE THE SPACE NEEDLE'S REVOLVING RESTAURANT, VIEWERS CAN TAKE IN THE CITY SKYLINE AS WELL AS THE CASCADE MOUNTAINS TO THE EAST AND THE OLYMPIC MOUNTAINS TO THE WEST.

Bill's favorite sports were the ones in which you were always moving—fast! Bill loved to water-ski, ice-skate, swim, and downhill-ski.

In sixth grade, Bill seemed to lose interest in school. Bill Sr. and Mary saw that their son needed a change. They decided to send him to a private school named Lakeside at the beginning of seventh grade. It turned out to be a great decision. The school pointed Bill's life in a new direction.

Chapter 2
Lakeside Whiz Kid

Bill was the smallest boy in his seventh-grade class at Lakeside School. Lakeside was then an all-boys school for grades seven through twelve.

Teachers at Lakeside worked hard to help kids develop their interests. Bill excelled in math and science. But he hadn't found his special interest yet.

One spring day in 1968, a teacher took Bill and some classmates to the new computer room. Actually, there was no computer in the computer room! At that time, personal computers didn't exist. There were only large mainframe computers that cost *millions* of dollars. Not even a private school like Lakeside could afford one.

So Lakeside had bought the next best thing—a Teletype machine. At first glance, it looked like a big electric typewriter. Beside it was a telephone that connected the machine to a mainframe computer in downtown Seattle.

The teacher showed
the boys how to type a
command. *Clackety-clack.*
The Teletype started punching
holes on a long spool of paper
tape. It made a terrible racket.
Soon the teacher's message was
speeding through telephone wires
to the computer several miles away.
In a little while, the machine typed back the
answer that it received from the computer.

Bill was amazed at what a computer could
do! He started to spend all his free time in
the computer room. He read every computer
manual he could find. And he learned computer
languages, such as BASIC. A computer language
is a code used to "talk" to computers.

Several other Lakeside boys became hooked on
computers, too. The boys learned from each other
as they went along. Lakeside teachers had planned

EARLY COMPUTERS

EARLY COMPUTERS WERE GIANT MACHINES. THE UNIVAC, A COMPUTER FROM THE 1950S WHEN BILL GATES WAS YOUNG, WAS A MONSTER WEIGHING OVER FOURTEEN TONS. IT SPREAD OUT OVER 350 SQUARE FEET OF FLOOR SPACE. DESPITE ITS ENORMOUS SIZE, THE UNIVAC HAD ABOUT AS MUCH MEMORY AS A HANDHELD CALCULATOR DOES TODAY.

COMPUTERS IN THE EARLY 1960S WERE RUN BY TRANSISTORS. THE UNITS, CONNECTED BY CABLES, WERE AS BIG AS REFRIGERATORS. THEY

HAD TO BE KEPT IN AIR-CONDITIONED ROOMS
ON RAISED FLOORS WHERE TRAINED OPERATORS
OVERSAW THEM AROUND THE CLOCK. THESE
MAINFRAMES COST MILLIONS OF DOLLARS. ONLY
UNIVERSITIES, GOVERNMENT AGENCIES, AND HUGE
CORPORATIONS COULD AFFORD THEM. OTHER
BUSINESSES AND SCHOOLS PAID A FEE TO USE
MAINFRAME COMPUTERS ON A TIME-SHARING
BASIS.

to learn about computers and then teach the kids. However, it worked the other way around. Bill and his pals became the experts. Then they taught the teachers!

At Lakeside, Bill had discovered his life's passion. Now his sharp mind had a focus. Computers, computers, computers!

Chapter 3
Learning a New Language

The whiz kids formed a computer club. They called themselves the Lakeside Programmers. Soon many of the boys were writing their own programs. A *program* is a set of instructions for the computer. Bill was thirteen when he wrote his first program. It was for playing tic-tac-toe.

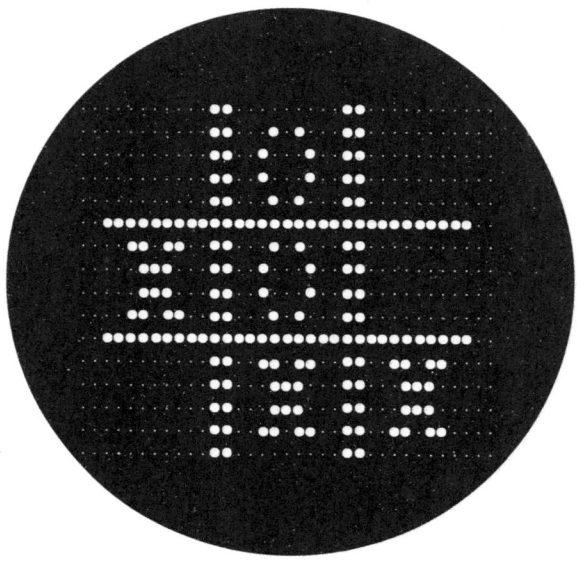

For a boy like Bill, who liked to test himself, the computer was the perfect challenge. Every single program was a test. Would it work? Only if Bill had written the code right—exactly right. If not, the computer would make mistakes. Wrong data in, wrong data out.

Bill was two years younger than most of the other boys in the club. At one point, the members decided Bill was too young. They also thought he was hogging time at the Teletype machine. So Bill got kicked out of the club. Not for long, though. Bill knew things that nobody else had figured out yet. The other boys needed him, so they asked Bill back.

Computer time wasn't free. General Electric, the owner of the mainframe computer, charged Lakeside School eighty-nine dollars a month to rent the Teletype. In addition, they charged students eight dollars an hour for computer time. This was expensive. At that time, you could buy sixty-six comic books for eight dollars!

At first the Lakeside Mothers' Club paid the computer fees. Soon, though, the Mothers' Club ran out of money. Now the students had to pay for their own time using the computer.

Bill's parents paid for his costly schooling. But they told him he had to pay for computer time himself.

So what did Bill do?

He found a job! Years later, Bill joked that his parents drove him into business.

A new company had just opened in Seattle. Its name was Computer Center Corporation. It had a mainframe computer. The boys nicknamed the company C-Cubed for the three *C*s in its name. Few people understood computers then. So C-Cubed turned to the bright boys at Lakeside School and made a deal. The boys could use the company's mainframe computer for free if they searched out "bugs," or flaws, in its programs.

For Bill and his friends, this job was paradise. Here was a huge computer worth millions of dollars. It was under their control.

The boys had to work during off-hours—at
nights and on weekends—when the company
staff didn't need the computer. So after school,
eighth-grader Bill often caught a bus and rode to
C-Cubed. Many nights, he and his buddies stayed
until midnight. If Bill missed the late bus, he had
to walk three miles home.

The following year, C-Cubed went out of business. But Bill's career was just beginning. At age fifteen, Bill went into business with one of the other Lakeside Programmers. His name was Paul Allen. The boys wrote a computer program called Traf-O-Data. It measured traffic flow in Seattle. Eventually, Traf-O-Data earned the boys $20,000!

Bill and Paul Allen were opposites. Paul was two years older, soft-spoken, and somewhat shy. Bill was outspoken and ready to argue to make a

point. Oddly, the two boys became fast friends. They shared a love of computers. They also both respected each other's ideas and intelligence.

Bill and Paul talked for hours and hours about the future of computers. The possibilities seemed endless! They believed computers had the power to change people's lives.

During his junior year, Bill got another programming job—from his own school. Lakeside had just merged with an all-girls school. The class schedules were too complicated to make by hand. Some teachers tried to write a computer program for schedules. But when they failed, they asked Bill and a classmate to help. In exchange, the boys would get about $5,000 worth of free computer time.

Happy for the challenge, Bill wrote a program that ran Lakeside's schedule like clockwork. An extra perk came with the job. Bill found a way to put himself into classes with lots of girls!

In 1973, Bill graduated from
Lakeside School. By now, he was
on the tall side. Everyone
at Lakeside knew who he
was. He got ready to
start college at famous
Harvard University.

Lakeside School had
been life-changing for Bill.
There, he had discovered
computers. He had started
his first business and earned
thousands of dollars. He

had also met Paul Allen, a friend who became his future business partner. Before too long, the two Lakeside Programmers would put their minds together and do something that had never been done before.

Chapter 4
Opportunity Knocks

During his first year at Harvard, Bill was busy with college classes. Then, in the middle of his sophomore year, Bill read a magazine article that changed his life. Paul Allen was working in Boston at the time. He saw the article first. These words blazed across the cover of *Popular Electronics* in January 1975: WORLD'S FIRST MINICOMPUTER KIT.

Right away, Paul rushed over to Harvard to show Bill the magazine. Bill understood why Paul was so excited. This was amazing news! People could now buy a kit to build a small computer. It could do many of the same things as a huge mainframe. Its name was the Altair 8800. In actuality, the Altair wasn't the world's first minicomputer. But it cost less than $400. So it was the first one cheap enough for hobbyists, people who like to do things themselves.

The Altair didn't look at all like computers do today. About the size of a microwave oven, it looked like a black box with switches and lights. There was no keyboard. There was no screen.

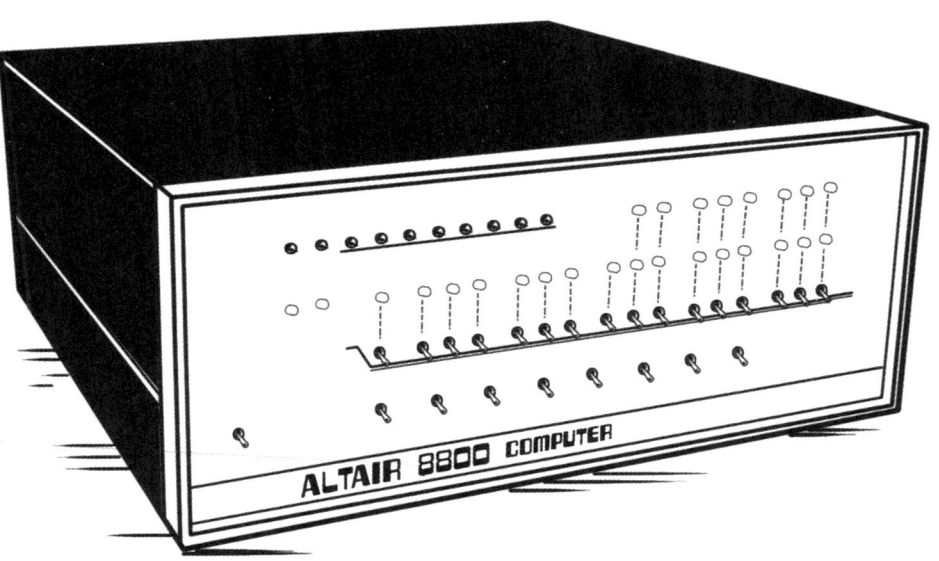

Plus, you had to put the Altair together yourself! Even once the computer was assembled, buyers wouldn't have much. They would only have the *hardware,* the "hard" parts of the computer that you can touch. But there was no software to go with the Altair. *Software* is the language program that tells a computer what to do. Without software, a computer can't do a thing. A computer without software is like a car without gasoline.

Bill and Paul were struck with a powerful idea. They would write software for this new machine. Both of them were excellent programmers. They had the energy. They had the skill. They knew they could do it!

Bill called the company that made the computer. It was Micro Instrumentation and Telemetry Systems (MITS). The company was located in Albuquerque, New Mexico. Bill told the head of MITS, Ed Roberts, that he and his partner

were writing language software for the Altair. Bill asked if MITS was interested in seeing it.

Sure, said Roberts. He agreed to meet with the boys in a month or so.

Yikes! Bill had claimed that their program was nearly done. In reality, he and Paul hadn't even started!

For about the next eight weeks, Bill and Paul worked like mad. The challenge was huge. They didn't even have an Altair to work on! MITS was behind in filling its orders. But the boys did have the instructions for the Altair. They could use them to build a *simulator*—a program that could "trick" a big computer into acting like a small one. In that way, they could use a mainframe computer to test out their new code.

Paul set to work building the simulator. Bill took charge of designing the software. He'd think hard before writing anything. Paul saw Bill "pacing and rocking for long periods before jotting on a yellow legal pad."

Bill had to juggle his college classes with this new project. Something had to give. For Bill, it was sleep. Often he'd work late into the night. Paul later described Bill during that time: "He'd be in the middle of a line of code when he'd gradually tilt forward until his nose touched the keyboard.

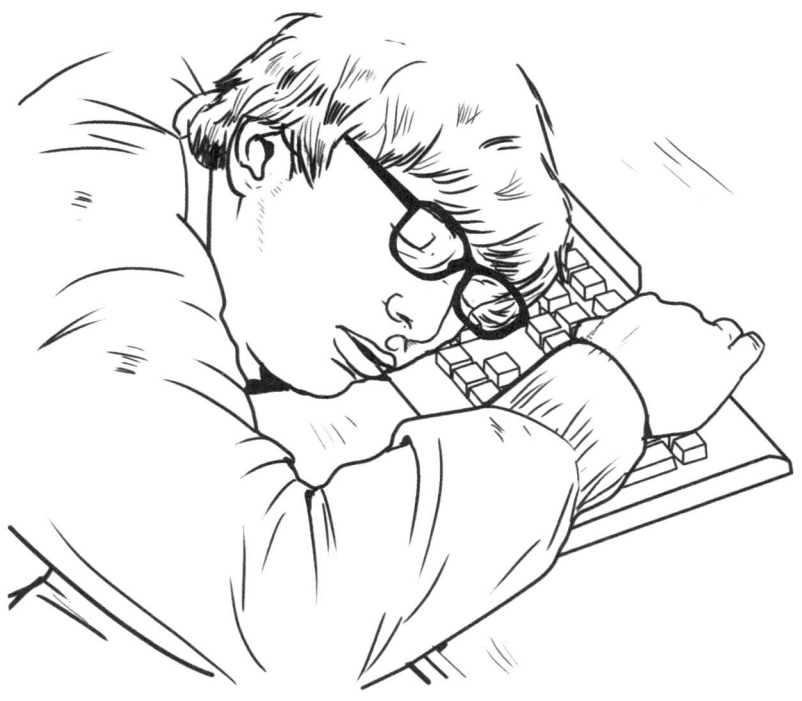

After dozing an hour or two, he'd open his eyes, squint at the screen, blink twice, and resume precisely where he'd left off."

As the deadline at MITS drew near, Bill lined up another friend from Harvard to help out. Just in the nick of time, the program was ready.

Paul was chosen to travel to Albuquerque and show the program to Ed Roberts. The boys had worked so hard! Now their dreams were on the line.

When Paul got to MITS, Ed Roberts brought him to a messy table. There sat the little Altair,

quiet and lifeless. Paul got ready to do a test run
of their program for Ed. He felt tense as he loaded
it. Their software had never been tried on a real
Altair before! Would it work? Was the code right?
Paul held his breath and put through the first
command:

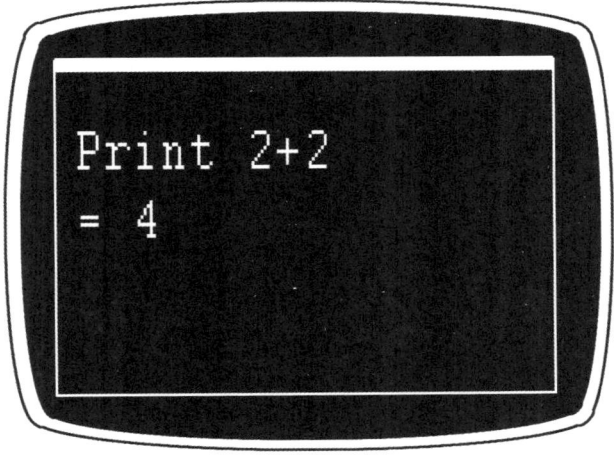

"PRINT 2 + 2."
Instantly, the computer shot back the answer:
"4"!
Success!

Minutes later, Ed Roberts decided to buy the program. Bill Gates and Paul Allen had created the very first programming language for a microcomputer.

Bill was only nineteen years old.

Chapter 5
Microsoft Is Born!

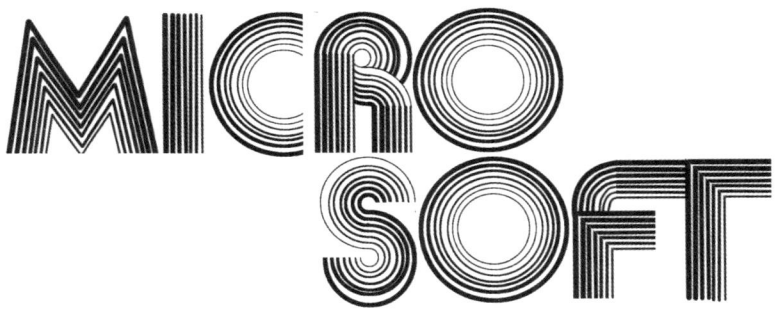

Now that they had a deal with MITS, Bill and Paul needed a name for their business. They decided to call it Micro-Soft because they were writing *soft*ware for *micro*computers. (*Micro* means *small*.) In less than a year, they dropped the hyphen. Bill was president and chairman of Microsoft, and Paul was vice president.

At first, the company was no more than a name. Paul took a full-time job at MITS as head of their software development. He was living in Albuquerque. Bill stayed at Harvard. Yet both boys dreamed of doing more with Microsoft.

So in 1975, Bill took a leave of absence—a "time-out"—to join Paul in Albuquerque. With Paul working part-time, the boys began new projects for Microsoft. Bill's parents did not want him to drop out of college. Reluctantly, Bill went back to Harvard. But his heart and mind just weren't in school. They were back in Albuquerque in the computer business that he and Paul had started.

Bill sensed that the computer world was at a major turning point. New computer chips had become available that could store lots of information on tiny wafers. Bill thought microcomputers were going to become big—really big. Here was his chance to do something important, and the moment to act was *now*! So he left Harvard again. This time he never went back.

Bill returned to Albuquerque and threw himself into his business. Soon Paul joined him full-time. He and Paul adopted a slogan for Microsoft: *A computer on every desk and in every home.* That was just a wild dream in the late 1970s. It seemed an impossible goal. But the partners set about making it happen.

By now the Altair was a success. Other companies were starting to make microcomputers, too. Like MITS, they only made hardware. Only one company, Apple, made both the hardware and software for its microcomputer. Microsoft was ready to make software for all the other companies.

Today we take software companies for granted. But as Steve Jobs once said, "Bill started a

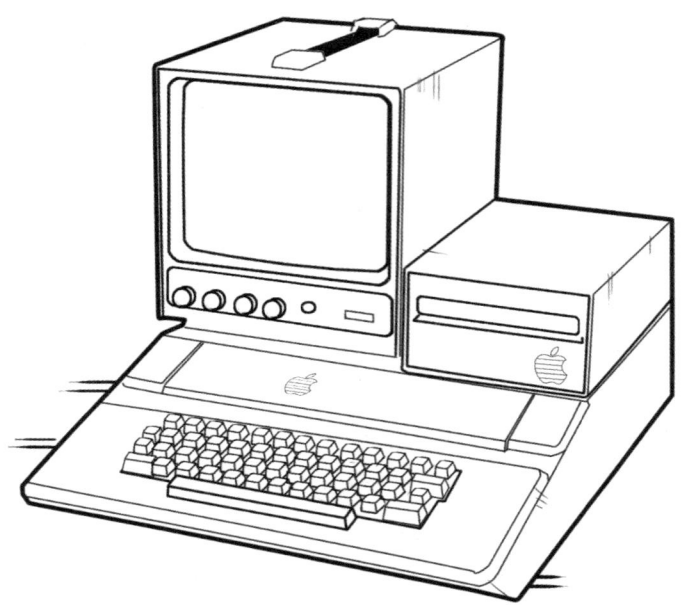

software company before anyone even knew what a software company was."

In the early days of Microsoft, Bill and Paul both did a little bit of everything. But Bill's keen business sense made him Microsoft's leader. He went on the road to drum up new business. He helped manage the staff. In addition, he wrote the code for the new software. More programmers were hired as Microsoft grew. But Bill remained the chief one. For years, not a single line of code went out of Microsoft until Bill went over it.

Often, Bill worked all day and most of the night. One morning a newly hired secretary arrived at the office and found a man lying under an office desk. She wanted to call the police. Laughing, the other employees told her that it was just Bill, sleeping after an all-nighter.

Bill expected people at Microsoft to work late nights and weekends like he did. Most of the employees didn't seem to mind. They were young, smart, and driven, too. And they believed in microcomputers.

For fun, Bill drove his fancy Porsche 911. Often he'd take coworkers out in the middle of the night for fast rides on the desert roads outside town.

In 1979, Bill and Paul decided to move their

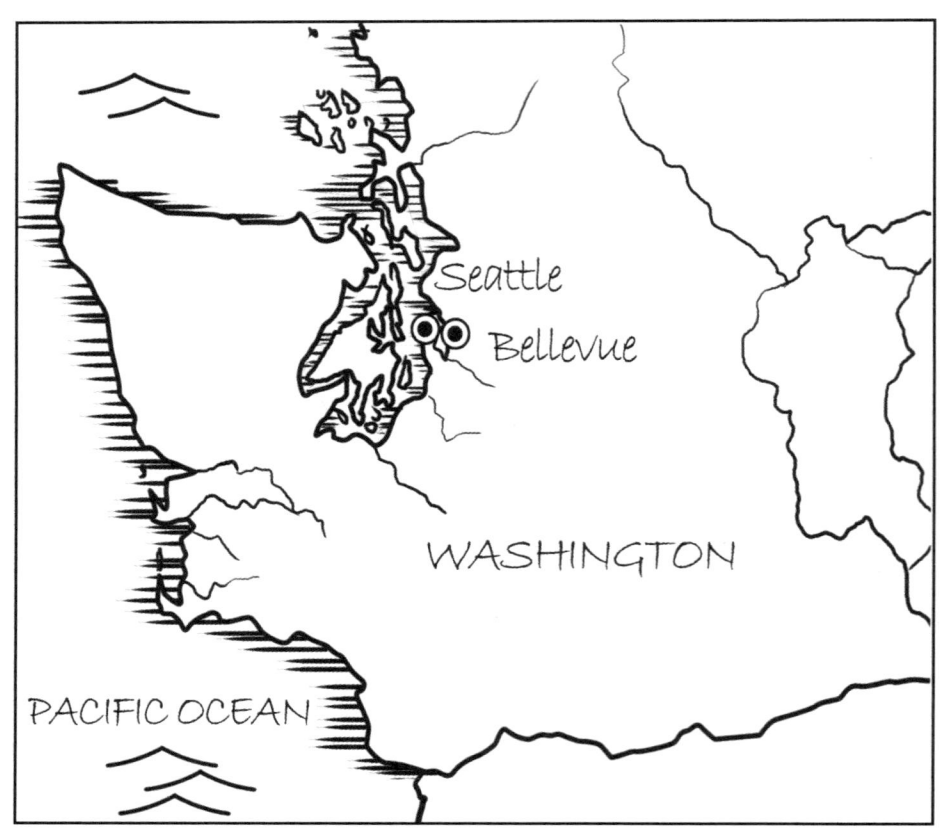

company. The desert city of Albuquerque was out of the way for clients. Plus, Bill and Paul wanted to be in green country again, close to family and friends. So Microsoft moved to Bellevue, Washington, near Seattle.

Before leaving Albuquerque, the small Microsoft staff posed for a picture. Eleven out of the thirteen original employees were in the shot.

There was hope and determination in their young faces. Maybe they were looking ahead to their own bright future.

Chapter 6
A Big Deal

Bill had always had a nose for business. When he was ten, Bill couldn't afford to buy an expensive new baseball glove. So he paid his sister Kristi five dollars to use her baseball glove whenever he needed it. To seal the deal, Bill wrote a contract and made his sister sign it!

In 1980, Bill got ready to sign a major contract with IBM. It would make Microsoft a much more powerful company.

IBM was then the world's biggest maker of computers—huge *mainframe* computers. Now

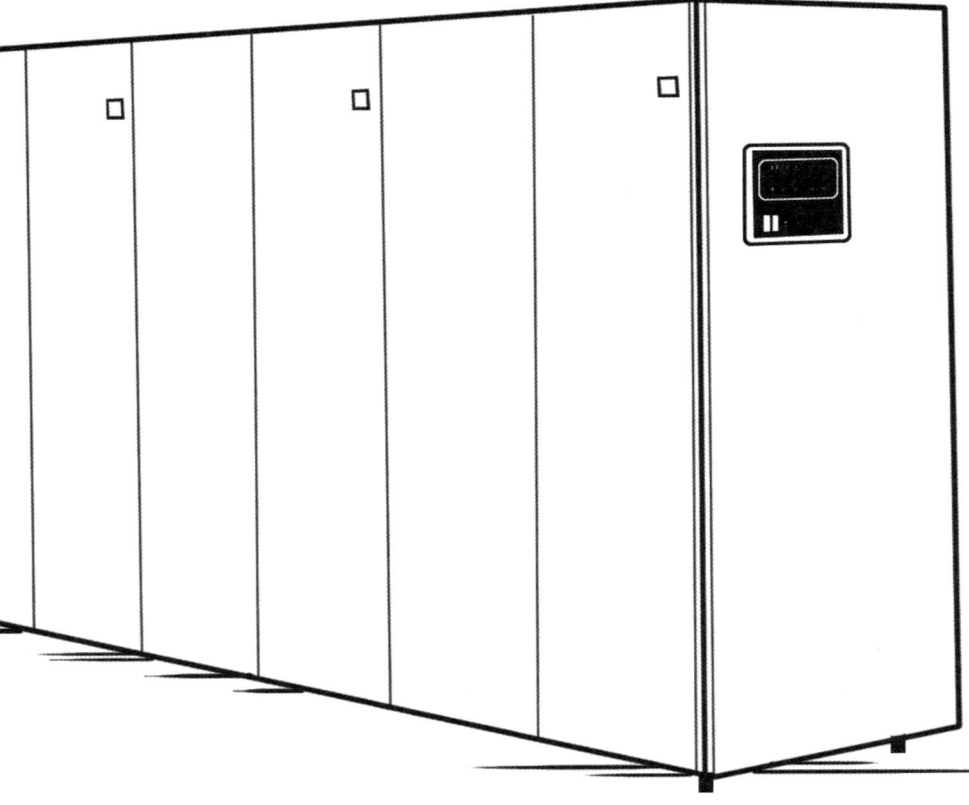

they wanted to get into the small-computer business, too. So they went to Microsoft.

What an opportunity! Bill was twenty-four years old at that time, and thirty-two people were working at Microsoft. In contrast, giant IBM employed well over three hundred thousand people.

At first glance, Bill looked too young to be taken seriously by the businessmen at IBM. However, they soon saw how much he knew about computers. IBM decided to hire little Microsoft to develop the language and operating system for its new personal computers. An *operating system* is the most important software on a computer. It runs the keyboard, the monitor, and all the other software programs. A computer without an operating system is like a car, all gassed up and ready to go, but without a driver.

For nearly a year, Microsoft worked to create the software for IBM. And in 1981, IBM was ready to roll out its first microcomputer. It was called a personal computer—PC, for short. Each and every PC was run by MS-DOS. *MS* stood for

Microsoft; *D* stood for *disk*; and *OS* stood for *operating system*.

Sales skyrocketed! Soon other hardware companies were making clones of IBM's personal computer. A *clone* is a copy. That meant that Microsoft could sell versions of MS-DOS to all these companies, too.

Before long, MS-DOS became the standard operating system for computer users around the world. All these users could share files. There was now a global language—and it lived inside computers.

As a result, growth at Microsoft was explosive. By the end of 1981, the company had 130 employees. By 1983, there were nearly 500. Bill no longer knew everyone by name.

Still, he stayed right in the middle of the action. He was a very hands-on boss.

At meetings with Bill, programmers had to be prepared. Bill's brain was something like a hard drive. It stored a huge amount of information, about both computer programs and the business world. In addition, Bill could see the big picture. He caught on very quickly to other people's ideas. If there were holes in a plan, Bill saw those, too. Sometimes he'd shout at a programmer, "That's the stupidest thing I ever heard!"

New workers were sometimes taken aback by Bill. Paul later wrote that Bill "with his intellect and foot-tapping and body-rocking . . . came on like a force of nature."

Yet Paul saw that Bill respected programmers who stood up to him and defended their ideas. What mattered to Bill was finding the best answer to problems. If he challenged new ideas, it was to make sure all the details had been carefully thought out. If so, Bill would end the meeting—no matter how much he had shouted—by quietly saying okay.

Workers who stayed at Microsoft came to understand and appreciate the big boss. The company's success spoke for itself. Clearly, Bill knew what he was doing. Employees were glad to be at a cutting-edge company.

And besides, Bill had a sense of humor and fun. He set up summer picnics where teams of Microsoft employees competed in contests and games. It was just like the Cheerio Olympics of Bill's youth.

The company was losing a very important person, though. In 1982, Paul Allen found out

that he had Hodgkin's disease. This is a kind of
cancer that very often can be cured. Paul had been
feeling a lot of pressure at work. Fighting over
ideas was fun for Bill. But for Paul, fights were
stressful. When he was healthy again in 1983, he
decided to leave Microsoft.

Bill wrote Paul a letter before he left. "During the last fourteen years we have had numerous disagreements," he wrote. "However, I doubt any two partners have ever agreed on as much."

In 1984, Bill appeared on the cover of *TIME* magazine for the first time. He was now the face of Microsoft. From then on, whenever people thought of Microsoft, they would think of Bill Gates.

Chapter 7
On the Fast Track

If Bill liked to move fast, he was in the right industry! In the 1980s, the computer industry was changing at a dizzying pace. There were new companies, new ideas, and new products. Competition was fierce!

In 1985, Microsoft came out with their newest software update: Windows. What made it so different was a little pointer called a *mouse*. The

little device had actually
been invented years
before. But this was
the first time that

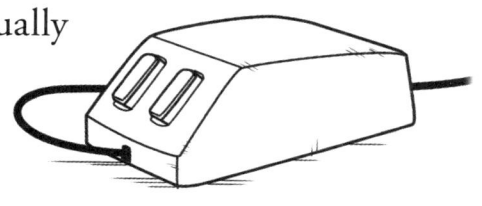

most computer owners had ever used one. The
mouse drove a system that radically changed the
old PC way of doing things.

Before, PC users had to memorize commands
and type them on a keyboard. But with Windows,
users could just point to pictures—
icons—on the computer screen.
Click the mouse and an entire
program would open. Point and click
on another icon and another program would open
that ran at the same time! Having more than one
"screen" open at a time was why the new software
was called Windows.

Xerox had been the first computer company to
use a mouse, followed by Apple. After Microsoft
came out with Windows, Apple sued the company

for taking parts of their design. Microsoft won in court when they showed that their product was truly different from Apple's.

Windows was *user-friendly*, a new term meaning it was easy to use. Computers were changing what many words meant. Programmers liked to take familiar words and apply them to computers. Words such as *menu, tool, dock, paste*—and, of course, *mouse*—got brand-new meanings.

Work at Microsoft was more intense than ever—and so was Bill. Success didn't make him relax. No matter how well his company did, Bill was always looking over his shoulder to see who was gaining on him. There was hardly time to *think*! So Bill started going on a retreat once a year, just to reflect on fresh ideas and the future of computers. He called this time-out "Think Week." It gave him time to read about new ideas in the field. Many of the ideas were turned in by his staff. Bill realized that his managers also needed breaks. So Bill made Think Week a yearly "holiday" for them, too.

In 1986, Bill took Microsoft public. *Going public* means that anybody—not just workers at a company—can buy shares of stock in that company. *Shares*, small pieces of a company, are sold on the stock market.

Shares in Microsoft sold at lightning speed. Overnight, Bill Gates (and cofounder Paul Allen) became millionaires. By 1987, the value of the stock had risen so high that Bill became a billionaire. He was just thirty-one years old, the youngest self-made billionaire up until then.

A billion dollars ($1,000,000,000) is so much money that it's almost hard to fathom. In his book *How Much Is a Million?*, David M. Schwartz figured out that it would take over ninety-five years to count out loud to one billion. And that's without taking any breaks to eat or sleep!

Put another way, if you made $1 billion in a year, you'd be earning about $19 million a week, $475,000 an hour, and $8,000 a second!

Eight years after becoming a billionaire, Bill was listed as the richest man on earth! He kept this top spot for many years—from 1995 to 2007, and again in 2009. Bill's fortune was worth well over $50 billion. How long would it take to count *that*? Go figure it out!

Chapter 8
Family Life

Hugely rich and successful, Bill showed no desire to get married. His business remained his first love.

Then at thirty-two, Bill met an attractive, dark-haired manager at a Microsoft picnic. Her name was Melinda French. When he talked

to her, Bill could tell that Melinda was smart, independent, and fun-loving. It didn't take long before the two were going out together.

Melinda, nine years younger than Bill, had grown up in Dallas, Texas. She was the number one student in her high school class. At Duke University, she got degrees in both computer science and economics. Then she went on to get a graduate degree in business. Soon after that, Melinda was hired by Microsoft.

Right from the start, others could see that Melinda was a good match for Bill. She shared his interests and understood his business. Whenever

they were seen together, the couple seemed to be laughing and talking spiritedly.

On New Year's Day 1994, Bill and Melinda were married on the island of Lanai in Hawaii.

The wedding was world news. However, Bill and Melinda had privacy by renting all the hotel rooms on the island and hiring all the helicopters. That way, photographers couldn't fly over the wedding and take pictures.

Bill was thirty-eight. He had stayed single longer than most men. Now he found that married life with Melinda suited him to a tee. His personal life began to take on new meaning.

In 1995, the couple took off on a trip to explore the world, going everywhere from China

to Africa. The next year, their first child was born. The Gateses named their daughter Jennifer Katharine. Three years later in 1999, they had a son, Rory John. And in 2002 their third child, Phoebe Adele, joined the family.

Bill had started to build a new house even before getting engaged to Melinda. In 1997, the fifty-five-thousand-square-foot dream house was ready for the Gates family to move in.

The mansion was built at the top of a steep hill overlooking Lake Washington outside Seattle. To save trees from being cut down, the home was mostly made from salvaged, or old, lumber.

To save energy and keep the house safe during earthquakes, it was built into the hillside.

The style of the house is very modern. And, of course, the technology is state-of-the-art. Guests can wear a badge with a tiny microchip that contains information about their favorite things.

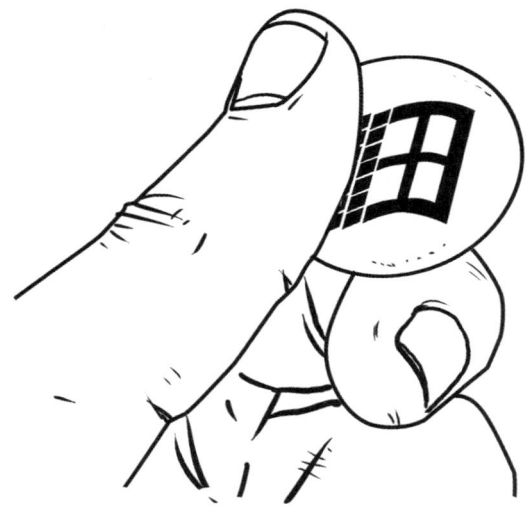

The chip sends signals. When a guest enters a room, his favorite music plays. The lighting and room temperature automatically adjust to suit the person's tastes. Even his favorite art is displayed on

the walls! (The works of art appear on screens that
are controlled electronically.)

The estate has everything one could wish for.
There is a game room, a movie theater, and a
gym. A sixty-foot-long indoor pool plays music
underwater. It also has a glass wall that swimmers
can dive beneath to get outside. There they find a
boathouse, a dock, and a guesthouse.

Of all the beautiful rooms, Bill's favorite is
the enormous library. A bookcase behind a secret
wall in the library holds a treasure that's over five
hundred years old. It is a handwritten
notebook by the genius
Leonardo da Vinci.
Bill paid over $30
million to buy it.

Despite the mansion's grand scale, the main living quarters of the family are fairly modest, with seven bedrooms. Only their closest friends are invited to this part of the house. Even though their fame is worldwide, the Gateses guard their privacy. Bill and Melinda want their children to have normal, happy childhoods like they both had.

LEONARDO DA VINCI (1452–1519)

"LEONARDO WAS ONE OF THE MOST AMAZING PEOPLE WHO EVER LIVED. HE WAS A GENIUS IN MORE FIELDS THAN ANY SCIENTIST OF ANY AGE AND AN ASTONISHING PAINTER AND SCULPTOR." THAT'S HOW BILL DESCRIBED LEONARDO DA VINCI.

LEONARDO LIVED FIVE HUNDRED YEARS AGO IN ITALY. HE IS MOST RENOWNED FOR HIS PAINTINGS, WITH MASTERPIECES SUCH AS THE *MONA LISA* AND *THE LAST SUPPER*. BUT HE HAD

A BRILLIANT SCIENTIFIC MIND, TOO. LEONARDO DESIGNED THINGS THAT WERE HUNDREDS OF YEARS BEFORE THEIR TIME—SUCH AS A FLYING MACHINE AND A SUBMARINE!

LEONARDO FILLED NOTEBOOKS WITH HIS BRILLIANT IDEAS AND DRAWINGS. TWENTY-ONE OF THEM SURVIVE TODAY. IN 1994, BILL GATES BOUGHT ONE OF LEONARDO'S SCIENTIFIC NOTEBOOKS. EACH YEAR HE SENDS IT ON A WORLD TOUR TO DIFFERENT MUSEUMS, WHERE OTHERS CAN ENJOY THE NOTEBOOK.

Chapter 9
Facing Challenges

A new kind of surfing became popular in the 1990s. Instead of surfing ocean waves, people began surfing the Internet. The Internet is a worldwide web of linked computers. By surfing the Internet—going from site to site—users can learn about almost anything without leaving their chairs.

In its early days, Bill did not realize the importance of the Internet. The Internet frontier attracted lots of other businesspeople, though. New Internet companies sprang up almost overnight. One company was Netscape, which made a popular browser. (A *browser* connects computer users to the Internet and the sites they want to visit.)

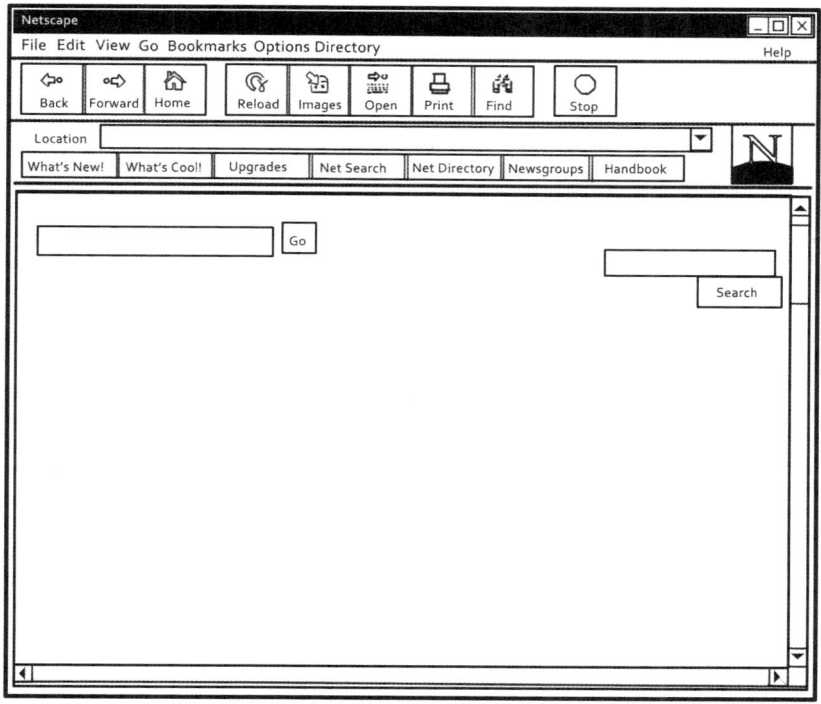

Suddenly Bill realized his mistake. He was jolted into action. He wrote a long memo to his employees. The subject line was *The Internet Tidal Wave*. In the memo, Bill declared that the Internet was "the most important single development" since the PC. He told everyone at Microsoft to make the Internet a top priority.

In 1995, Bill launched Microsoft's first Internet browser. It was called Internet Explorer. By that

time, Netscape had already cornered more than 90 percent of browser sales. Microsoft had a lot of catching up to do.

Bill charged ahead by bundling Microsoft's browser with its operating system. Anyone who bought Windows got Internet Explorer for free. Because of this, Internet Explorer zoomed ahead and overtook Netscape.

This time, however, Bill's bold actions got him into legal trouble. In 1998, the US Department of Justice took Microsoft to court.

Why?

It's not illegal, after all, to have a very popular product that everyone wants to buy. But it is against US law to prevent competition from another company making a similar product. According to the government, that's what Microsoft was doing. At that time, about 80 percent of PCs ran Microsoft's operating system. Now they would automatically be using Internet

Explorer, too. Companies such as Netscape had no way to compete. According to the lawsuit, that wasn't fair.

The trial was a terrible blow to Bill. But many people had no sympathy for him or his company. During the rise of his computer empire, Bill had made many enemies. His critics said Bill wanted to win at all costs. In the business world, he was seen as a big bully. Many people thought Bill was arrogant. Even at the trial, he seemed defiant.

Bill Gates

Bill said that being sued by his government was the worst thing that had ever happened to him. To Bill, the legal charges against his company made no sense. He pointed out that Microsoft spent billions each year to research and develop new products. Punishing a company for success would be a threat to innovation, Bill claimed.

The court did not agree with Bill. In 2000, a judge ordered Microsoft to be split in two: one company for operating systems and a second for software development. Later, the ruling was overturned. Finally, in 2002, the case was settled in Microsoft's favor. Although Microsoft had to change some of the ways it did business, the giant company could stay in one piece.

The trial lasted four years. But through it all, Bill kept showing up to work each day with his usual energy.

Why did he even bother to work when he had so much money? Someone asked that very question and sent it in to a newspaper column that Bill wrote. The column was called Ask Bill.

Bill wrote back: "The answer is simple: I do what I find interesting and challenging, and I think I have the best job in the world."

Nonetheless, Bill was no longer thinking about Microsoft morning, noon, and night. Serious world problems had caught his attention. Bill had begun to think he should use his mind, power, and money to help solve those problems.

Chapter 10
Sharing the Wealth

The English language has a special word
for a person who donates a lot of money to the
common good: *philanthropist* (say: fih-LAN-thro-
pist). After years of making enormous amounts of
money, Bill began giving enormous amounts away.

Important people in Bill's life inspired him to
be generous. His mother, Mary Gates, had been
active in charity work before she died in 1994.
Bill's friend Warren Buffet also urged him to

WARREN BUFFET

WARREN BUFFETT IS ONE OF THE WEALTHIEST MEN IN THE WORLD—AND ONE OF THE MOST GENEROUS. BUFFETT'S COMPANY IS CALLED BERKSHIRE HATHAWAY. IT DOES NOT MAKE PRODUCTS THE WAY MICROSOFT DOES. INSTEAD, BERKSHIRE HATHAWAY BUYS OTHER COMPANIES, COMPANIES THAT ARE RUN WELL AND WHOSE PRODUCTS WARREN BUFFETT LIKES, SUCH AS SEE'S CANDIES, GEICO CAR INSURANCE, AND FRUIT OF THE LOOM UNDERWEAR. BUT WARREN BUFFETT IS NOT ONLY KNOWN FOR HIS SMART BUSINESS MIND. HE ALSO IS INCREDIBLY GENEROUS. HE HAS PROMISED TO GIVE AWAY 99 PERCENT OF HIS WEALTH. IN 2006, WARREN BUFFETT PLEDGED A GIFT OF STOCK WORTH ROUGHLY $30 BILLION TO THE BILL & MELINDA GATES FOUNDATION TO BE GIVEN OVER TWENTY YEARS.

WITH BILL GATES, HE ALSO CREATED THE GIVING PLEDGE, THROUGH WHICH ALMOST SEVENTY OTHER BILLIONAIRES HAVE PROMISED TO GIVE AT LEAST HALF OF THEIR MONEY TO CHARITY.

donate his fortune to good causes. But probably the biggest influence on Bill was his wife, Melinda. She was a down-to-earth woman who believed in helping others.

Bill and Melinda talked about what to do with their large fortune. They decided to give 95 percent of it away. Bill said, "I believe with great wealth comes great responsibility—a responsibility to give back to society."

	2000
Pay to the order of Bill & Melinda Gates Foundation	
Twenty-Eight Billion Dollars	/ 100 Dollars
Polio Research	*Bill Gates*

In 2000, the couple created the Bill & Melinda Gates Foundation. A *foundation* is like a business that is set up to give away money. Bill and Melinda donated billions of dollars from their personal fortune to their foundation. Now they asked themselves this question: "How can we do the most good for the greatest number with the resources we have?"

Bill had read a report that said millions of children in poor countries were dying from diseases that no longer existed in richer countries. They were diseases such as polio, malaria, and yellow fever. So many of these children could be saved by getting a vaccine that cost just a few cents!

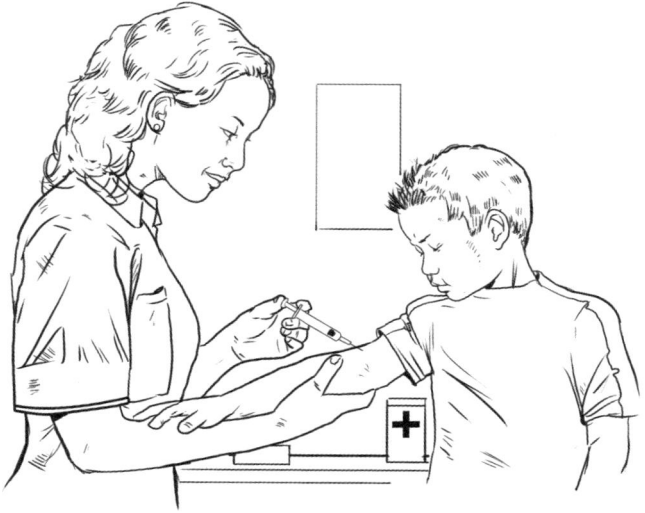

Bill showed the information to Melinda. "We were shocked!" Bill told a TV interviewer. "If you believe that every life has equal value, it's revolting to learn that some lives are seen as worth saving and others are not. We said to ourselves: 'This can't be true. But if it is true, it deserves to be the priority of our giving.'"

Bill stepped down as CEO of Microsoft in 2000. He handed over the job to his college friend Steve Ballmer, who had been with Microsoft since 1980. Then, in 2006, he announced that he was getting ready to retire from Microsoft to work full-time at the Bill & Melinda Gates Foundation.

POLIO

IN THE FIRST HALF OF THE TWENTIETH CENTURY, POLIO WAS ONE OF THE MOST DREADED DISEASES OF CHILDHOOD. ALTHOUGH SOME WHO CAME DOWN WITH POLIO SUFFERED NO LASTING EFFECTS, IT OFTEN LEFT CHILDREN PARALYZED OR CRIPPLED. ADULTS COULD CATCH POLIO, TOO. PERHAPS THE MOST FAMOUS VICTIM OF POLIO WAS U.S. PRESIDENT FRANKLIN D. ROOSEVELT. AFTER CATCHING THE DISEASE AS AN ADULT, HE WAS CONFINED TO A WHEEL-CHAIR AND COULD ONLY WALK A FEW STEPS WITH THE AID OF HEAVY LEG BRACES.

SIXTY YEARS AGO, POLIO WAS AT ITS PEAK, AFFLICTING ALMOST SIXTY THOUSAND PEOPLE IN THE UNITED STATES IN THE YEAR 1952 ALONE. THEN VACCINES WERE DISCOVERED THAT PREVENTED POLIO. (ONCE SOMEONE CAUGHT THE DISEASE, THERE WAS NO CURE.) ONE VACCINE WAS CALLED THE SALK VACCINE, AFTER DR. JONAS SALK. IT WAS INJECTED INTO A PATIENT WITH A NEEDLE.

ANOTHER VACCINE WAS THE SABIN VACCINE, NAMED AFTER DR. ALBERT SABIN. IT CAME IN LIQUID FORM; PATIENTS ONLY HAD TO DRINK A SMALL AMOUNT. THE VACCINES WERE TRULY WONDER DRUGS; VERY QUICKLY THEY WIPED OUT POLIO IN THE WESTERN HEMISPHERE.

HOWEVER, IT STILL RAMPAGED IN POOR COUNTRIES WHERE PEOPLE COULD NOT GET OR AFFORD THE VACCINE. IN 1988, MORE THAN 350,000 CHILDREN WORLDWIDE SUFFERED FROM THE DISEASE. THAT YEAR THE GLOBAL COMMUNITY TOOK ON THE GOAL OF ENDING POLIO ALTOGETHER. BILL AND MELINDA GATES HAVE POURED FUNDS INTO THE CAUSE. IN HIS 2011 ANNUAL FOUNDATION LETTER, BILL GATES REPORTED THAT THE NUMBER OF CASES HAD GONE DOWN BY 99 PERCENT. BUT HE ADDED, "THE LAST ONE PERCENT REMAINS A TRUE DANGER." CASES COULD CROP UP AND SPREAD AGAIN. "WE ARE SO CLOSE, BUT WE HAVE TO FINISH THE LAST LEG OF THE JOURNEY," BILL URGED. "WE NEED TO BRING THE CASES DOWN TO ZERO."

June 27, 2008, was Bill's last full-time day at Microsoft. He was fifty-two years old and had headed his company for thirty-three years.

In 1975, the staff of Microsoft had been just its two founders—Paul Allen and Bill Gates. Today Microsoft employs around ninety thousand people.

Back then, a typewriter sat on every office desk. Today, in the United States, after the

software revolution that Bill led, a computer sits atop almost every office desk and is in almost every home. The flying logo of Windows opens on more than seventy-five million of these computers around the world.

Chapter 11
Life Today

In March 2010, Bill was bumped down to the second-richest man in the world. Bill said, "Obviously I don't care." It had happened because he had given $28 billion to his foundation by then.

Today, Bill throws himself into work, just as always. With his usual intensity, he works to lift people out of extreme poverty, cure diseases, and improve US education, especially in inner cities.

As before, Bill loves his job. "The day-to-day part of it is fun," he said. He and Melinda travel to faraway spots in the world to get a firsthand view of problems. One day recently, he found himself in a tent with a tribal leader in a remote village where no one had ever heard the name Bill Gates.

Other days find Bill talking to scientists about
their complex research. The work requires Bill to
master all sorts of scientific knowledge in order to
decide which ideas should get money.

Every day, Bill faces countless hard decisions.
He needs to draw on the business skills he
developed as the CEO of a large company.
Sometimes the foundation takes risks that don't
work out. Bill realizes that's part of the job. He
and Melinda wrote guiding principles for their
foundation. One was "We take risks, make big
bets, and move with urgency. We are in it for the
long haul."

Bill also meets with government officials all around the world. In 2011, the global economy was sinking. Many countries were cutting back on their aid programs. Bill fought against these cutbacks. "The world's poorest will not be visiting government leaders to make their case," he pointed out, "so I want to help make their case."

Leaders tend to listen to Bill. Bill gives them sensible reasons for continuing aid programs—the kinds of reasons he would have listened to earlier in his career. He said, "I understand the need for belt-tightening in downturns." But he pointed out that in many countries, aid is only about 1 percent of public spending. "That amount of money isn't causing the world's fiscal problems," Bill said. He added that there was a huge payback for giving. It made countries more stable and less violent.

Bill and Melinda have seen firsthand some of the terrible problems in the world. Yet Bill often says, "Melinda and I are optimists." That means they have great hope for the future. Bill believes that new advances in the high-tech world can "give us a chance we've never had before to end extreme poverty and end death from preventable disease."

In his free time, Bill still enjoys reading. Recently he read a four-hundred-page book about vaccines—and enjoyed it! A reporter asked him if that made him a geek. "I plead guilty," said Bill with a smile. "Gladly."

Other pastimes Bill likes are playing tennis and the card game bridge. But as Bill once said in a newspaper interview, he's "not a sit-on-the-beach type." To him, that's boring. Fun to Bill is being

with Melinda and the kids. No matter how busy he gets, Bill says that "the kids are a big part of my schedule."

And work itself is fun to Bill. That's one of the reasons he has been able to accomplish so much.

It is easy to see why *TIME* magazine named Bill one of the "Most Influential People of the Twentieth Century." And in 2007, he finally got

Bill Gates
"One of the Most Influential People of the 20th Century"

a degree—an honorary one from Harvard. Bill spoke at the Harvard graduation. He joked to his father in the audience, "I've been waiting more than thirty years to say this: 'Dad, I always told you I'd come back and get my degree.'"

How will history judge Bill Gates? Will he be remembered as much for his philanthropy as for his leading role in the computer age?

Don't bother asking Bill. He's too busy working!

TIMELINE OF
BILL GATES'S LIFE

1955	Born on October 28 in Seattle, Washington
1962	Reads the entire *World Book Encyclopedia*
1968	Encounters his first computer, a Teletype machine
1973	Graduates from Lakeside School
1974	Begins college at Harvard University
1975	Writes the software for the Altair 8800 with Paul Allen Leaves school to start Microsoft with Paul
1980	Microsoft signs major deal with IBM
1983	Paul leaves Microsoft
1987	Becomes a billionaire
1994	Marries Melinda French on the island of Lanai in Hawaii Mother, Mary, dies
1996	Daughter Jennifer Katharine is born
1999	Son, Rory John, is born
2000	Creates Bill & Melinda Gates Foundation to fight poverty and polio Steps down as CEO of Microsoft
2002	Daughter Phoebe Adele is born
2007	Receives an honorary degree from Harvard University

TIMELINE OF THE WORLD

Dr. Jonas Salk begins vaccinating children against polio —— **1954**

Sputnik is sent into orbit by Soviet Union —— **1957**

The Space Needle in Seattle is displayed at the city's World's Fair —— **1962**

Neil Armstrong is the first person to walk on the moon —— **1969**
The Woodstock rock music festival goes on for three days in August

Popular Electronics announces the world's first minicomputer kit —— **1975**

Pac-Man video game is released in Japan —— **1979**

E.T.: The Extra-Terrestrial comes out in movie theaters —— **1982**

Wreck of *Titanic* is discovered —— **1985**

The World Wide Web is created —— **1991**

The first photograph is uploaded to the Internet —— **1992**

Tiger Woods wins his first Masters Tournament —— **1997**

Terrorists attack the Twin Towers in New York City and the Pentagon in Washington, DC —— **2001**

Facebook is first launched —— **2004**

Barack Obama is elected president of the United States —— **2008**

BIBLIOGRAPHY

Allen, Paul. **Idea Man: A Memoir by the Cofounder of Microsoft**. New York: Portfolio, 2011.

* Aronson, Marc. **Up Close: Bill Gates**. New York: Viking, 2008.

Gates, Bill, "Harvard Commencement Speech Transcript," **Network World**, June 8, 2007, www.networkworld.com/news/2007/060807-gates-commencement.html.

Gates, Bill, "Innovation with Impact: Financing 21st Century Development" (report by Bill Gates to G20 leaders), November 3, 2011, www.thegatesnotes.com/Topics/Development/G20-Report-Innovation-with-Impact.

* Lesinski, Jeanne M. **Bill Gates: Entrepreneur and Philanthropist**. Minneapolis: Twenty-First Century Books, 2009.

* Lowe, Janet. **Bill Gates Speaks: Insight from the World's Greatest Entrepreneur**. New York: John Wiley & Sons, 1998.

"Transcript: Bill Moyers Interviews Bill Gates," PBS, May 9, 2003, www.pbs.org/now/transcript/transcript_gates.html.

"Values." Bill & Melinda Gates Foundation. www.gatesfoundation.org/about/Pages/values.

* Books for young readers